Alexander Graham Bell

Jacqueline Langille

Four East Publications Ltd.
P.O. Box 29
Tantallon, Nova Scotia B0J 3J0

Copyright 1989
All rights reserved

1st printing 1989   8th printing 2003
2nd printing 1990
3rd printing 1992
4th printing 1996
5th printing 1999
6th printing 2000
7th printing 2001

edited by Hilary Sircom
design by Paul McCormick
printing and typesetting by
    Print Atlantic
    Dartmouth, Nova Scotia, Canada

Acknowledgements

The publisher wishes to express his appreciation for the generous financial support of the **Nova Scotia Department of Tourism and Culture** and the **Canada Council.**

The publisher and author have received the assistance of the staff of the Alexander Graham Bell National Historic Park, especially Mr. Jack Stephens and Miss Aynsley MacFarlane. Their help with both visuals and text has been invaluable to us.

We also wish to thank the Mulgrave Road Co-op Theatre for their interest and help, especially Shauna Graham.

All photos courtesy of Environment Canada — Canadian Parks Service Alexander Graham Bell National Historic Park except for the photo on page 46, which is courtesy of Kent Nason.

Richard Rogers, Publisher

Canadian Cataloguing in Publication Data

Langille, Jacqueline, 1966 -
    Alexander Graham Bell

(Famous Maritimers)
(Bibliography: p.
ISBN 0-920427-22-7

1. Bell, Alexander Graham, 1847-1922.
2. Inventors — United States — Biography.
3. Inventors — Canada — Biography.
I. Title, II. Series

TK6143. B45L36 1989   621.385'092'4   C89-098600-2

Preface

There is for all of us a fascination in discovering how people lived in the past. Most adults are familiar with the questions, "What was it like when you were growing up?" and "What did you do when you were my age?" The series is intended to address this interest and to make available to young people some of the material previously found only in books directed towards the adult market. Although the biographies have been kept brief, the bibliographies will suggest reading for those who would like to do further research.

These Famous Maritimers who were pioneers and innovators in their day are our local heroes and heroines; the contribution they made to our way of life is recorded in our museums and historic homes. We hope that this series will increase awareness of our Maritime heritage both for those who already live here and for the visitors who may wish to stay awhile in order to get to know us and our history better.

Hilary Sircom
General Editor

Contents

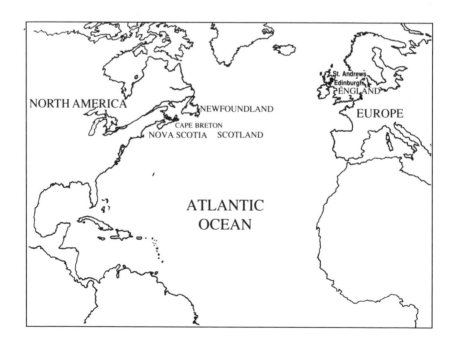

Introducing Alexander Graham Bell 1847-1922

After 1876 the world became a smaller place as the invention of the telephone made it possible for the human voice to travel across vast distances. Today we can have instant communication with relatives, friends or business associates in any corner of the globe. Indeed the telephone may be considered one of the most important inventions of all time. Its inventor was a twenty-nine-year-old Scottish teacher of the deaf, named Alexander Graham Bell.

His work with deaf people led Bell to experiment with many different ways of communicating, and the ideas for the invention of the telephone were being formed while he was living with his parents in Brantford, Ontario. However, the first telephone conversations took place in the United States.

Bell became an American citizen, but he lived for much of his later years in Cape Breton, Nova Scotia. His success with the telephone made him rich and famous, and he was able to buy a summer home at Baddeck. There, for many years, he continued his experiments and, with his friends, carried on the work of the Aerial Experiment Association.

Bell did amazing work with kites, experimenting with the principles of flight. In his time, many of the world's leading scientists believed it was impossible for man to achieve powered heavier-than-air flight. Dr. Bell proved them wrong. He was never one to be swayed by the opinions of other people! He created many wonderful machines during his lifetime, a number of them being built and tried out at his Baddeck estate on the shore of the Bras d'Or Lakes.

Alexander Bell, Aged fifteen, at his father's country home on the outskirts of Edinburgh.

In Scotland: The Home of the Bells

There were three generations of Alexanders in the Bell family. Young Aleck Bell was named for the grandfather on whose birthday he was born on March 3, 1847 in Edinburgh, Scotland.

Grandfather Alexander had been first a shoemaker in St. Andrews, then an actor, and finally a teacher of correct speech (elocution). Father, Alexander Melville, known as Melville, was also a reader of Shakespeare and teacher of speech, and had become famous for his invention of Visible Speech. In this system, every sound made by mouth, throat, teeth and lips had a special symbol, could be used in any language, and could even help deaf people learn how to speak. The three Bell children, Melville James, Alexander and Edward Charles, grew up learning Visible Speech and were living proof of how well the system worked.

Whenever Melville Bell held a lecture to demonstrate his methods, he took his three boys with him. He would send them out of the room and then ask the audience to make different sounds. These he translated into Visible Speech symbols on a blackboard. When his boys returned, each would read the symbols and would take turns making the sounds. The

Alexander Melville Bell, 1819-1905, a speech therapist and teacher of elocution.

audience was always amazed that the boys could make these almost exactly, even to the sound of sawing wood, or words from foreign languages.

At home, Aleck's mother taught the boys reading, writing, history, geography and music. As they became ten, their father sent them away to a private school. Aleck never enjoyed school because he had so many interests that he found it hard to settle down and study just what his teachers wanted.

On one of his vacations, Aleck met his father's friend, Alexander Graham. Liking the sound of this name, and wanting to distinguish himself from the other two Alexanders, his father and grandfather, Aleck announced that his new name was Alexander Graham Bell.

Having watched his father at work, Aleck was also interested in speech, and he began to wonder why the family dog could not speak. He knew that dogs have tongues, lips, throats and teeth almost like humans, so why could they not talk? His father pointed out that people learn to talk when they are babies so if he could go about teaching the dog as if it were a child, then maybe it could make noises that would sound like talking. Aleck worked with the dog for months, teaching it different sounds by holding its mouth until it learned almost a whole sentence. With a treat and a little encouragement, the dog would make noises like this: "ow-ah-oo-ga-ma-ma". With a little imagination this can sound like "How are you, Gran' mamma?" The Bells' talking dog soon became a sensation over the whole countryside.

Edinburgh Royal High School students about 1858. Alexander Graham Bell stands second row from the top, fourth from the left.

Mr. Bell was always interested in people who claimed they could make machines that could talk and would take his boys to see them. Usually these machines were either a trick, or did not really produce sounds like talking. After one especially amazing lecture, Bell asked his two older boys if they thought they could make a talking machine. He said he would reward whichever of them did best. The boys decided to work together and, with all the knowledge they had gained from their father, built their machine as much like the human head as possible. Melville made the throat and voice box, while Aleck tried to construct a skull and mouth. They made teeth, a palate, and a speaking tube, trying to copy the way a human voice is produced. They blew air through the throat, while Aleck molded the lips. The sound that came out was a "ma" sound. When they did it fast, it sounded so much like a baby crying that people came out of their

Grandfather Alexander Bell, 1790-1865. A specialist in speech therapy, he exerted a strong influence on his grandson's development.

apartments in the building to see what was the matter. Their father was so pleased with the boys' work, that he gave them both a prize.

At fourteen, Aleck graduated from school; although he was no scholar, he had never failed anything. His parents were not really impressed with his performance so, hoping the old gentleman would have a good influence, they sent him to England to spend a year with his grandfather, Alexander Bell.

The year in London certainly had the desired effect. His grandfather made him dress like a gentleman, taught him the classics, and paid for piano lessons. Indeed Aleck became so good on the piano that he wanted to become a professional pianist. He had hated the routine of study at his grandfather's house but, by the end of the year, he knew how to work and had picked up much valuable knowledge. His grandfather had treated him like a man, and he had a hard time fitting back into family life in Edinburgh.

Young Melville was also feeling it was time to move from home and, although he was only 18 and Aleck 16, the boys applied for teaching jobs advertised in the local paper. At this point their father realized they were ready to take on some responsibilities, and he made Melville his own assistant while Aleck went to teach music and language at Weston Academy.

In 1865 Grandfather Bell died and, while young Melville remained behind to run his father's school, the rest of the family moved south to take over the business contracts Grandfather had made. The London weather with its fog and pollution proved unhealthy for Edward, the youngest son, who died of tuberculosis in 1867. Aleck had spent some time studying in Bath but soon moved to London to become his father's assistant. He worked so hard that he appeared to be much older than he really was. Meanwhile, in Edinburgh, Melville was also suffering from the strain of his heavy work-load and, in 1870, he died, also of tuberculosis.

Melville James Bell, Alexander's older brother.

In the New World: A New Life

Mr. and Mrs. Bell mourned the sad loss of their two sons and, realizing that Aleck was also far from well, were determined to save the life of their last son. Mr. Bell remembered the wonderful bracing climate of Newfoundland, where, as a young man, he had spent four years recovering from a serious illness, so he decided to move his wife, son and business to Canada.

Later that year they arrived in Brantford, Ontario, where they bought a house in Tutelo Heights. This was perfect for Aleck to rest and relax, breathe good clean Canadian air, and start a new life. Yet there were always demands on him. His father was asked to go to Boston to teach Visible Speech to the teachers of the deaf. Mr. Bell realized he could not be in two places at once but that his son could very well fill this position, so, in 1871, Aleck went off to teach in Boston. His teaching methods were much admired, and he was even given a class of his own at the university.

Aleck's work with the deaf was most important to him all his life. He was doubtful about the value of sign language and believed that if only deaf children could learn to speak, they could function in the world like everyone else.

Alexander Melville Bell (at right) and Mrs. Bell (wearing cap) in front of the family home at Tutelo Heights, Brantford, Ontario. The Bells emigrated to Canada in 1870 after losing two sons to tuberculosis, a dreadful disease which was afflicting so many in industrialized Britain.

One of Aleck's early pupils was Mabel Hubbard, a young girl who had become deaf at the age of five after a serious illness. She had learned to lip-read with a private tutor and entered the class of Professor

Mabel Gardiner Hubbard at age thirteen or fourteen. At five years of age, the future Mrs. Bell was stricken by an attack of scarlet fever which left her permanently deaf.

Bell in Mohawk garb. Bell studied the Mohawk language using his father's system of Visible Speech. He became so fluent that he was initiated into the tribe with full ceremonial rites.

Bell to improve her speech, for, although she could already talk, she could not remember hearing her voice and it sounded strange. She did well in his class, and soon Aleck realized he was becoming very fond of his pupil.

Another special pupil was a small boy named Georgie Sanders. Aleck taught him to understand speech and gave the boy confidence to come out of his shell and live a normal life. This was like a miracle to his grateful family.

Besides teaching, tutoring and lecturing Aleck was also doing experiments with telegraphy. He was trying to invent a device he called a harmonic telegraph and also a multiple telegraph, hoping to be able to send more than one message at a time over a telegraph line. He was always concerned with the lack of real communication and hoped that his experiments might change the world. With all this work it was no wonder he needed to return to Brantford, to regain his strength in the summer time.

However, even there he did not rest for long. He had always been interested in the Mohawk Indians, whose territory was all around Brantford, and now he spent his free time learning their language and customs. The Mohawks admired Alec (now spelling his name without the "k") so much that they made him an honourary member of the tribe, presented him with a real Indian outfit, and taught him their war dance. After this, whenever he was very happy, Alec would do the Mohawk Indian war dance, complete with war cries!

Back in Boston, one of the most interested supporters of Bell's experiments in telegraphy was Gardiner

Mabel's parents, Mr. and Mrs. Gardiner Greene Hubbard, enjoy tea at Twin Oaks, their Washington home, July 1877. Mr. Hubbard was a founder and first president of the National Geographic Society.

Greene Hubbard, Mabel's father. Alec spent many Sunday afternoons at the Hubbard home explaining his experiments and discussing his hopes for the future. The more time he spent there, the more he realized how much he cared for Mabel ("May" as she was known to her family). He admired her lip-reading ability, her courage and her beauty.

Alec was used to being with deaf people as his own mother was so hard of hearing that she had been using a large black ear trumpet for years, but somehow Mabel Hubbard made him nervous. Soon he knew it was because he was in love with her. His years of illness had made him appear very old and the Hubbards, thinking Professor Bell to be close to forty, did not wish to have their young daughter upset by a romance with an "older man". Alec was in fact only twenty-six! Soon things were smoothed over and Mabel and Alec (affectionately known as "Sandy") were engaged.

Meanwhile Mr. Hubbard also provided Alec with support, in the form of money for his experiments in telegraphy. At a workshop in 1874, Bell had met Thomas Watson and formed with him a partnership which would make history. Watson was able to provide the practical help Bell needed to make his ideas actually work.

At home, in Brantford, during the summer, Alec missed Mabel terribly but had plenty of time to think. He thought how wonderful it would be if people could talk across the same wires that carried telegraph messages and wondered if electricity could actually be used to send the sound of the human voice. By the time he returned to Boston he had in his head the idea for the invention of the telephone. Both Hubbard and Watson felt this was impossible but were caught up by their friend's enthusiasm and agreed to help him.

After two years of working hard with little success, and just as their money was running out, their efforts were finally rewarded. March 10, 1876, was a day to remember, as Thomas Watson heard Bell's voice over

Painting by W.A. Rogers showing Bell explaining a telephone instrument to his assistant, Thomas A. Watson. In this room at 5 Exeter Place, Boston, on March 10, 1876 the twenty-nine-year-old inventor spoke these historic words through the first telephone: "Mr. Watson, come here, I want you."

the wire saying, "Mr. Watson, come here — I want you". The very first telephone call was a cry for help. Bell had made the world a smaller place, by bridging the distance with a human voice. This was certainly an occasion for the war dance.

Alexander Graham Bell received a U.S. patent for his telephone but spent eighteen years fighting law cases against other inventors who claimed to have invented it first. Eventually he became a rich man from the telephone company started under his name, one which is still known world wide.

With the telephone such a success, Bell could now give up teaching and devote time to his other inventions. On July 11, 1877, he married Mabel and was never happier.

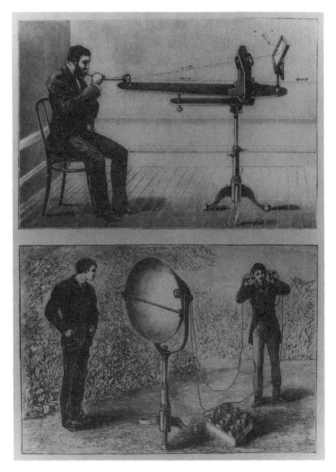

The Photophone. Developed by Bell and his associate, Charles Sumner Tainter, in 1879-80, the photophone transmitted voice over light beams.

Happy Days: The Beautiful Mountain

The Bells spent their honeymoon in Scotland and also travelled in England where Alec gave lectures about his invention. Because he was the expert on the telephone, the name of Alexander Graham Bell was known and respected throughout Europe, and his lectures were such a success that the couple decided to remain for awhile in England. Here, a year later, their first daughter, Elsie May, was born. A second daughter, Marian Hubbard, arrived soon after their return to North America in 1880.

The family settled down in a new home in Washington, D.C., and Bell continued with his experiments. The day Marian was born was also the day on which Bell heard the sound of a human voice carried by sunlight over a device he called a "photophone".

When, in the summer of 1881, President Garfield was shot by an assassin, Bell tried to invent a machine which would locate the bullet. Unfortunately his experiments were not successful, nor were the skills of the best doctors, and the President died in September of that year. However, Bell persisted with his idea and had soon invented an electric probe which could indeed detect bullets in the body. This invention earned him an honorary degree of Doctor of Medicine from the University of Heidelberg, an honour to be added to the many others he had received for his invention of the telephone. By the time he was thirty-four he was close to being a millionaire and was respected as a scientist of world renown.

Bell used the prize money awarded to him by France to start the Volta Laboratory where he did much of his later work. He continued to devote much of his time and energy to his projects for deaf children; the Volta Bureau provided services for the deaf and their families and carried out important research into the problem of hereditary deafness. More of Bell's money went into supporting the newly founded National Geographic Society and Mabel's father became its first president.

Bell had become an American citizen and was happy to call Washington his home. Two sons were born to the Bells but neither lived very long. This was most tragic for them as they both loved children, but they were comforted by watching their two beautiful girls grow up. The Washington summers were extremely hot, and this sort of weather had always bothered Bell; so he decided to try to find a place which would be cool and private where they could spend their summers.

In the summer of 1885 they set sail for Newfoundland, stopping on the way at Cape Breton Island. Here Bell found that the rugged cliffs, jagged coastline, large lakes and evergreen forests reminded him of his home in Scotland. They stayed in a pleasant lodge in Baddeck, relaxing, exploring and enjoying the scenery. When they set off again for Newfoundland, their ship ran aground and started to sink. Bell

Mr. and Mrs. Alexander Graham Bell sit for a formal family portrait with daughters Elsie May (left) and Marian in December, 1885.

helped to keep the passengers calm and kept their spirits up until finally they and the crew were rescued. The experience had been extremely frightening and, feeling that they could not take any more surprises after such a scare, the Bells cancelled the rest of their vacation and returned home.

In spite of this experience, the family returned to Baddeck the following year and rented a farm house. They spent the summer exploring the area, and Bell taught his daughters to swim in the cold waters of the inland seas, the Bras d'Or Lakes. Alec and Mabel went on canoe trips together or hiked on trails along the shores. On one such walk they discovered Red Head which rose high above the surrounding land with beautiful views in all directions. They fell in love with this spot and first built a temporary lodge there to serve as a summer home until, after several years, they were able to purchase all the land on the hill top. In 1892 they had built there a huge mansion which they called *Beinn Bhreagh* which is Gaelic for "beautiful mountain". By the following summer it was ready for the family to move in.

The Bells had found the perfect place for rest and relaxation and spent longer and longer vacations in Cape Breton, often staying well into the winter and indeed sometimes remaining for the whole year. Even here Bell continued with his experiments, having a laboratory built near the house. He would work until late, often till two or three in the morning; then he also enjoyed walking on the hills at night sometimes not returning until dawn. He would, as a result, sleep late in the morning often not getting up till noon.

Flock of sheep grazes behind Beinn Bhreagh Hall. In 1890, Bell began experiments in sheep breeding trying to create a breed of sheep that would consistently bear twins instead of single lambs. He hoped to increase the profits from sheep breeding in order to benefit the farmers of Nova Scotia. However, years of cross-breeding experiments brought only limited success.

When they built *Beinn Bhreagh*, Bell bought a flock of sheep. Careful records were kept while he experimented hoping to raise a breed which would have twins, triplets or maybe litters of lambs. He kept flocks of sheep for almost thirty years and actually developed a variety which usually had twins. He loved talking about his sheep, interested to see if people really knew anything about such a common animal. One of his favourite questions was, "How many teeth does a sheep have on its upper jaw?" Most people would guess any number from two to thirty-two, but Bell would always surprise them with the true answer — a sheep has no teeth on its upper jaw!

Bell loved spending time with his daughters and their friends. He taught them all to swim and paddle a canoe and directed them in family plays. They would write the script and build a set, and Mr. Bell would produce the whole show providing the music by playing the piano. His love for children lasted all his life and after his daughters had grown up, he entertained the children of his Baddeck employees and then his own grandchildren.

The Bells loved the waters of the Bras d'Or Lakes and had built a houseboat called the *Mabel of Beinn Bhreagh*. The family would go out for trips staying afloat for weeks on end, having food and other supplies brought out to them by boat. After several years of service, the *Mabel* was retired to blocks near the shore and Bell used her as a private office where he spent many hours. Each day he would dictate his thoughts and details of his experiments to his secretary, Arthur McCurdy, who would keep these notes in huge binders. Ever since others had tried to claim the invention of the telephone, Bell had insisted that complete and accurate records of his work must be kept.

Bell often retreated to the shelter of his houseboats where he could relax in a more private and leisurely fashion.

Everything Under the Sun: Bell's Experiments

Bell always considered himself to be first and foremost a teacher of the deaf and continued his work in the fields of sound and speech, but he had so many other interests. Among other experiments he carried out was one for distilling fresh water from sea water or from a person's own breath. He tried out ideas for air conditioning, submarines, rockets, x-rays, sonar and cancer treatments. His mind was always at work and one of his favourite subjects was flight.

Bell had always been interested in birds and used every occasion to study how they flew. Although other scientists had "proved" that heavier-than-air flight was impossible, he believed that one day man would be able to fly. Even though some of his ideas were laughed at, other scientists still came to visit him at Baddeck to share in his search for knowledge.

Two of the best known scientific brains of the United States happened to be visiting him at the same time one summer. These two men had never liked each other and were always arguing, so Alec tried to ease the uncomfortable situation by talking about something which would bother neither man. He

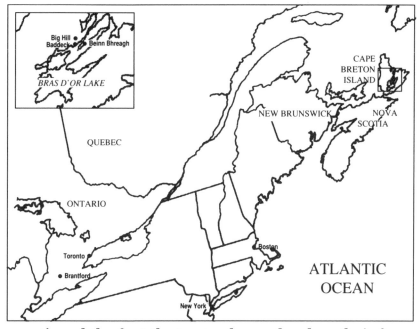

mentioned the fact that cats always land on their four
feet no matter how far they fall or from what angle
they are dropped. Both men knew a great deal about
physics and disagreed with Dr. Bell. He was abso-
lutely certain they would have to be shown the truth
before they would believe him, so he asked a worker to
gather up a few of the cats which were lounging
around the place. The Bells loved cats, so there were
always a dozen or so on the estate. With the help of a
stack of pillows and a balcony, the three world-
famous scientists spent the afternoon dropping the
protesting felines from a great height. No matter how
they were dropped, the cats always managed to twist
themselves in mid-air to land on the pillows on all
four feet. No cats were the worse for wear, and Bell's
two friends discovered an interesting fact which they
could actually agree upon.

In Washington the Bells lived a busy life of exacting work schedules and a social whirl of entertaining and parties. The Bells' home was known as a place of warm hospitality and Mabel was a queen of society. The girls were growing up and thinking about husbands and homes of their own. In 1897 Alexander Graham Bell became President of the National Geographic Society and, in a few years, he would install his own son-in-law as the Society's first employee in the position of editor of their magazine.

Back in Baddeck, in 1898, Bell started flying kites. He started with ordinary box kites which he made himself in his laboratory and flew in the wild winds above the *Beinn Bhreagh* cliffs. Then he tried

Bell and assistants inspect kites in the laboratory, around 1906.

Bell experimented with many forms of tetrahedral design in his kite trials. This huge ring kite was tested in 1907-08 but was abandoned after it showed a consistent tendency to sideslip and crash.

building larger kites by attaching box cells together but often these were so heavy that he could not get them off the ground. After much thought and experimentation, Bell found the best shape for his kite cells — the tetrahedron (a figure which has four triangular faces). These kites flew better, higher, longer and were much stronger. Bright red silk covered their surfaces, and they could be seen for miles flying in the breezes above the Bras d'Or Lakes.

To help him with his flying experiments Bell relied on four talented young men. Douglas McCurdy was the son of his secretary and a great friend of the Bell family. One year when he returned from university he brought with him a friend, F.W. "Casey" Baldwin, who became involved in the Bell experiments in flight for the next twenty years. Also involved were Glenn H. Curtiss, an expert in small engines, and Lieutenant Thomas E. Selfridge of the U.S. Army.

This was the time that rumours of the Wright brothers' first powered flight were being circulated and Mabel, tired of hearing all this talk of flying machines and wanting to see some action, put $20,000 of her own money into a special fund; that day the Aerial Experimentation Association was formed.

By 1908, they had built four planes, each of which was to find its place in aviation history. These planes were always called "aerodromes" by Bell. He was the head of the Association, but the actual work was done, and most of the ideas contributed, by the four younger men. On March 12, 1908, the first ever public flight of a heavier-than-air flying machine was performed by Casey Baldwin of Baddeck's AEA,

The Aerial Experiment Association. From left to right: Glenn Curtiss, John McCurdy, Alexander Graham Bell, Casey Baldwin and Lt. Thomas Selfridge.

---

taking off from Lake Keuka (which was covered with ice) in New York State. The plane was called *Red Wing* because the same red silk which had earlier been used on the kites covered her wings. This flight was acclaimed all over North America. However, the plane was not at all stable and crashed on her second flight.

The second "aerodrome" AEA put into the air had white sail cotton on her wings and was called *White Wing*. By now they had invented a hinged attachment, like an extra wing on the end of the main wing, which was to make the machine more stable by allowing the wing position to shift in the wind. The Bell group received the patent for this "aileron" which is still used on airplane wings today. *White Wing* was fitted with motorcycle wheels so she could take off from the ground and was flown by Baldwin.

Glenn Curtiss (right) and Thomas Selfridge (center) try out Red Wing's controls, March 9, 1908.

Casey Baldwin stands in centre of group assembled for maiden flight, March 12, 1908. Baldwin had the honour of piloting the initial flight, Selfridge having been called to Washington on military business. He flew the Red Wing 95.4 m at an altitude of 3 to 6 m. It was the first public flight anywhere by a Canadian.

The White Wing rises into the air at Hammondsport, May 18, 1908. Casey Baldwin piloted the plane over a distance of 83.7 m at an approximate altitude of 3 m.

She took off in front of a large crowd which included Bell who was deeply touched by the sight of his dreams come true.

Curtiss took this plane a record 1,017 feet in nineteen seconds but when McCurdy took her up, AEA had their second crash. One of the problems they experienced was that the cloth covering the wings was letting too much air through, so the wings of the third plane were "painted" with linseed oil. This machine flew like a dream and won the *Scientific American's* contest for flying the first public measured kilometre. Glen Curtiss won the trophy beating the Wright Brothers.

The fourth machine was the famous *Silver Dart*, so called because of the special silvery balloon fabric coated with rubber, which was used on the wings. After a couple of test flights she was shipped to Baddeck where McCurdy made the first flight in the

The Silver Dart is manoeuvred into takeoff position. Local villagers, many on skates turned out in force for the event.

British Empire, flying more than nine miles over the ice of Baddeck Bay.

While the AEA was flying in the USA, Bell had been working in Baddeck with Baldwin on the problem of getting a plane up off water which would be safer than taking off from land. They were experimenting with pontoons and hydroplaning surfaces but unfortunately were not successful at first. Meanwhile, Lt. Selfridge was killed when a plane he was flying with Orville Wright crashed in Virginia. Wright survived.

Canadian Aerodrome Company aircraft sit on the ice of Baddeck Bay, March 1910.

Mabel Bell gave a further $10,000 to continue the work of the AEA, and all the experimentation was now done at *Beinn Bhreagh* which became like a gigantic workshop with new buildings and an increased staff. Each trial was photographed and carefully dated; and in July, 1909, Bell started an estate newspaper called the *Beinn Bhreagh Recorder* which provides a fascinating chronicle of this early work in aeronautics. Copies of the *Recorder* are preserved in the Smithsonian Institute in Washington, D.C. and also in the library at the Alexander Graham Bell National Historic Park.

The Final Years: No Rest for the Inventor

In 1910, the Bells, joined by Casey Baldwin and his new wife, set off on a year's trip around the world. Everywhere they went, Bell was treated with respect and given many honours. Unable to take a rest, he carried his notebooks with him recording everything of interest which he saw. Often these notes were used later to enliven dinner conversations or to colour the speeches he gave.

On their return from this trip Bell and Baldwin set to work seriously on their designs for hydrofoils (boats which would travel over the water rather than through it) using a new propeller motor which they had discovered in France. The new machines were called "hydrodromes" abbreviated to H.D.

When, in 1914, Canada went to war and Baldwin was going to join the service, Bell suggested the young man should remain on coastal patrol so that they could work together to make the fastest patrol boat ever, which would be an asset to the Canadian Navy. After five years of experiments and trials of three of her unsuccessful hydrodromes, in 1919, the H.D.4 was ready to be tested. News people, the public,

Like a giant water bug, the HD-4 skims across the surface of Baddeck Bay. At a speed of about 32 km an hour, the hull was lifted clear of the water as if on stilts and the craft surged ahead, according to one visitor, "with an acceleration that makes you grip your seat to keep from being left behind."

friends and family all gathered to watch the high-powered motor boat. The H.D.4 thrilled the crowd as it raced across Baddeck Bay at 70.86 miles per hour, establishing a water speed world record which was not broken for ten years. Much of the work had been Baldwin's and, as always, Bell was quick to give credit where it was due.

Although Bell continued to work on his many projects, tying up loose ends and trying to finish half completed experiments, much of his time during his final years was spent with his family. Many of his happiest hours were when he was with his grandchildren.

It is interesting that Bell never let the telephone interfere with his private life. He said he had not invented it for people to use it to do things they would never do in person such as to disturb people at meal times or late at night. He felt this was very rude and would not answer it if his phone rang at these times. Also, he refused to say "Hello" and throughout his life, whenever he picked up the phone, announced himself by saying "Hoy, hoy!"

Dr. Bell made one last visit to Edinburgh and while there carried on his research into the Bell ancestors, which had been a life-long interest. The City of Edinburgh made him a Burgess and a Guild Brother, in recognition of his outstanding achievements. Now that his home town had finally given him its highest honour, his life seemed to have come full circle.

The doctors warned Bell that he was not well and should rest. However, he had never rested in his life and could not start now. He continued giving

Melville Grosvenor helps grandfather and assistants haul in a kite.

speeches, travelling and dictating his notes till the day he died. On August 2, 1922, Alexander Graham Bell died in his sleep at *Beinn Bhreagh*. As a sign of respect for the great inventor, all the telephone lines of North America kept a one-minute silence at 6:30 p.m. on the day of his funeral. Finally at rest, Bell was buried at the peak of his Beautiful Mountain, joined there only five months later by his beloved Mabel.

Beinn Bhreagh estate seen from the waters of the Bras d'Or Lakes.

From Past to Present

An inventor's work lives on to preserve his memory and certainly the telephone is the greatest monument to Alexander Graham Bell. Although it has been improved upon since his time, the basic concept of its operation remains exactly the same as his early invention.

Bell's memory is also kept alive by the National Geographic Society which celebrated its centenary in 1988 and devoted an article in the September issue of the magazine to Bell and his inventions. He would be proud of the society's record of scientific research and happy that the magazine, with its familiar yellow cover, continues to report on "the world and all that is in it". *The National Geographic* is found in homes, schools and libraries everywhere.

In Canada, the Bell home near Brantford, Ontario, has been preserved as a museum and contains many of the family heirlooms.

A two-act play about the Bells entitled *Beinn Bhreagh* has been performed by the Mulgrave Road Co-op Theatre of Mulgrave, Nova Scotia. This has been well reviewed and gives a tender portrayal of the relationship between the inventor and his wife.

John Dart and Wanda Graham star in the play **Beinn Bhreagh.**

In Cape Breton, Bell's estate is still to be found outside Baddeck, and he is buried there, but this is not the site of the museum which commemorates the life and work of the great inventor. A new building has been constructed from the tetrahedral shapes Bell was so fond of using in his kites. Thousands of visitors pass through this museum each year, pausing to marvel at the exhibits which display all the things Bell worked on at his Baddeck home, from kites, planes and hydrofoils to genetics and heredity.

The museum is a fitting monument to the genius of that American citizen and Canadian resident, inventor and teacher of the deaf, Alexander Graham Bell.

Bell Museum, Baddeck, Nova Scotia

Bibliography

Boettinger, H.M. *The Telephone Book*. Riverwood Publishers Limited, New York: 1977.

Costain, Thomas B. *The Chord of Steel*. Permabook, Pocket Books Inc., New York: 1963.

Green, Gordon. *The Silver Dart*. Brunswick Press Limited, Fredericton, New Brunswick: 1959.

Mackenzie, Catherine. *Alexander Graham Bell, The Man Who Contracted Space*. The Riverside Press, Cambridge, Mass.: 1928.

Parkin, J.H. *Bell and Baldwin*. University of Toronto Press, Toronto: 1964.

Stevenson, O.J. *The Talking Wire*. Julian Messner Inc., New York: 1947.

Waite, Helen Elmira. *Make a Joyful Sound*. Macrae Smith Company, Philadelphia: 1961.